ENGINEERED BY NATURE

THE GREAT BLUE HOLE

BY MARTHA LONDON

CONTENT CONSULTANT
ANDRÉ W. DROXLER, PHD
PROFESSOR
EARTH, ENVIRONMENTAL AND PLANETARY SCIENCES
RICE UNIVERSITY

Kids Core
An Imprint of Abdo Publishing
abdobooks.com

abdobooks.com

Published by Abdo Publishing, a division of ABDO, PO Box 398166, Minneapolis, Minnesota 55439. Copyright © 2021 by Abdo Consulting Group, Inc. International copyrights reserved in all countries. No part of this book may be reproduced in any form without written permission from the publisher. Kids Core™ is a trademark and logo of Abdo Publishing.

Printed in the United States of America, North Mankato, Minnesota
042020
092020

Cover Photo: Michael Conlin/iStockphoto
Interior Photos: David Doubilet/National Geographic, 4–5; Norbert Probst imageBroker/Newscom, 7; André Droxler, 8; NASA/Science Source, 10; Jad Davenport/National Geographic, 12–13; Spencer Sutton/Science Source, 15; Franko Maps, Ltd., 16–17; Brian J. Skerry/National Geographic, 18, 20–21; Jennifer Adler/National Geographic, 23; Andrew J. Martinez/Science Source, 24; Shane Gross/Shutterstock Images, 26; Red Line Editorial, 28–29; Shutterstock Images, 29

Editor: Marie Pearson
Series Designer: Megan Ellis

About the Consultant

André Droxler was born in Switzerland and had an early dream to become an oceanographer. He has studied many reefs all over the world since he moved to the United States in 1978.

Library of Congress Control Number: 2019954248

Publisher's Cataloging-in-Publication Data

Names: London, Martha, author.
Title: The Great Blue Hole / by Martha London.
Description: Minneapolis, Minnesota : Abdo Publishing, 2021 | Series: Engineered by nature | Includes online resources and index.
Identifiers: ISBN 9781532192883 (lib. bdg.) | ISBN 9781098210786 (ebook)
Subjects: LCSH: National parks and reserves--Belize--Juvenile literature. | Natural monuments--Juvenile literature. | Sinkholes--Juvenile literature. | National parks and reserves--Juvenile literature. | Landforms--Juvenile literature.
Classification: DDC 910.202--dc23

CONTENTS

The Great Blue Hole is very wide and deep.

CHAPTER 1

DOWN IN THE DEEP

A team of scientists and explorers is working to map the inside of the Great Blue Hole in Belize. The team climbs into a submarine. The submarine has a large, clear ceiling. Water burbles over the machine as it begins its slow dive.

At first the water looks bright blue. Coral branches out from the rock ledges. Sharks and fish swim slowly around. When the group reaches 40 feet (12 m), they see the first ledge. Here, the hole becomes a little narrower. It starts to get darker.

They sink deeper and deeper. Fewer animals swim around. Below 90 feet (27 m), the hole gets wider and darker. The team uses the submarine's lights to see the surroundings. There are caves with **stalactites** and **stalagmites**. These formations are a sign that the Great Blue Hole used to be a dry cave.

Eventually, the submarine reaches about 300 feet (90 m). It looks like there is a cloud in the water. A **toxic** gas spreads out like

Divers can explore the Great Blue Hole's stalactites and stalagmites.

a blanket. It blocks light from the surface. Beneath the blanket, there is no oxygen or living things. It is completely black.

Shells and other debris are mixed with the silt at the bottom of the hole.

The submarine finally reaches the bottom at 410 feet (125 m) deep. The bottom is covered in fine silt. Silt is made up of tiny pieces of material smaller than sand, but larger than clay.

A Sinkhole

A blue hole is an underwater sinkhole or cave. Its opening faces the water's surface. From above, it looks like a dark-blue circle. The Great Blue Hole is in the western Caribbean Sea. It is in the Lighthouse Reef. This reef is an atoll, or ring of coral. Lighthouse Reef is part of the Belize Barrier Reef System. A barrier reef is a **coral reef** that runs along a coast. It is separated from the mainland by water.

The Belize Barrier Reef

The Belize Barrier Reef is one of the largest reefs in the world. The reef is 180 miles (290 km) long. Many vulnerable and endangered animals such as the American crocodile and the manatee live near the reef.

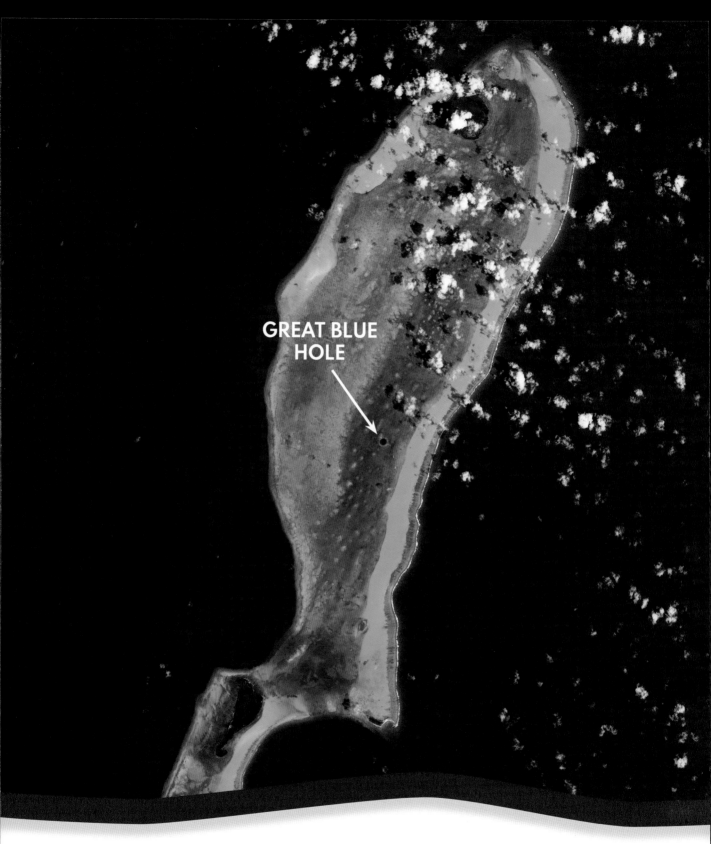

GREAT BLUE
HOLE

The Great Blue Hole is at the center of
Lighthouse Reef.

The Great Blue Hole is one of the largest blue holes on Earth. It is 980 feet (300 m) wide. It is 410 feet (125 m) deep. Scientists study this hole to learn more about how it formed. They dive deep in submarines to take samples and measurements. This information helps them learn about the hole and Earth's past.

Further Evidence

Look at the website below. Does it give any new evidence to support Chapter One?

Explorations inside the Great Blue Hole

abdocorelibrary.com/great-blue-hole

Today, there are dry sinkholes in Belize that are similar to the Great Blue Hole.

CHAPTER 2

ABOVEGROUND TO UNDERWATER

The Great Blue Hole in Belize was not always an underwater hole. It used to be part of a large, dry cave system. Earth's climate has changed many times. The cave has also changed.

The most recent cold period was about 20,000 years ago. Much more ice covered land. Because a lot more of Earth's water was in the form of ice on land, sea levels were much lower. The sea levels were about even with the floor of the Great Blue Hole. Lighthouse Reef was an island. Over thousands of years, a cave formed in the location of the Great Blue Hole. Eventually its ceiling collapsed to form a sinkhole.

The Bottom of the Hole

The bottom of the Great Blue Hole has a layer of silt. Storm waves stir up silt from the shallow seafloor around the hole. Some of the silt settles at the bottom of the Blue Hole.

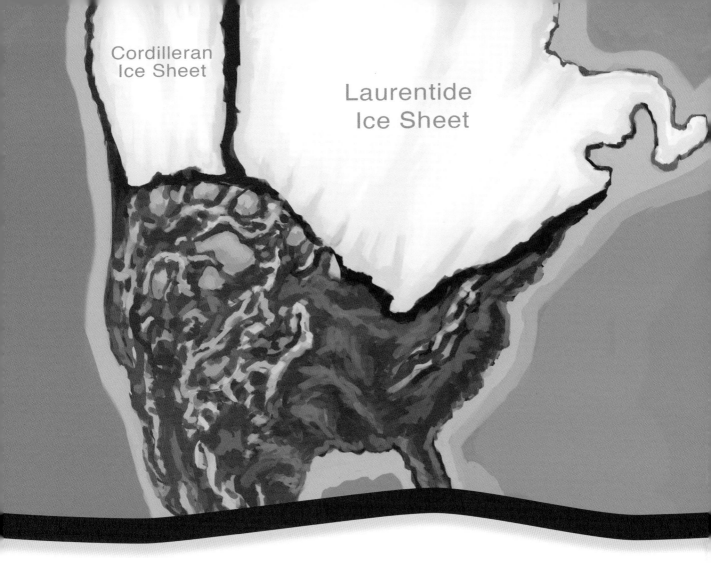

Cordilleran
Ice Sheet

Laurentide
Ice Sheet

During the last ice age, a lot of Earth's water was stored as glaciers in North America.

The cold period ended approximately 19,000 years ago. As the climate warmed, a lot of ice melted. The water flowed into the ocean. Ocean levels began to rise. The sinkhole flooded. The Great Blue Hole had formed.

Great Blue Hole Cross Section

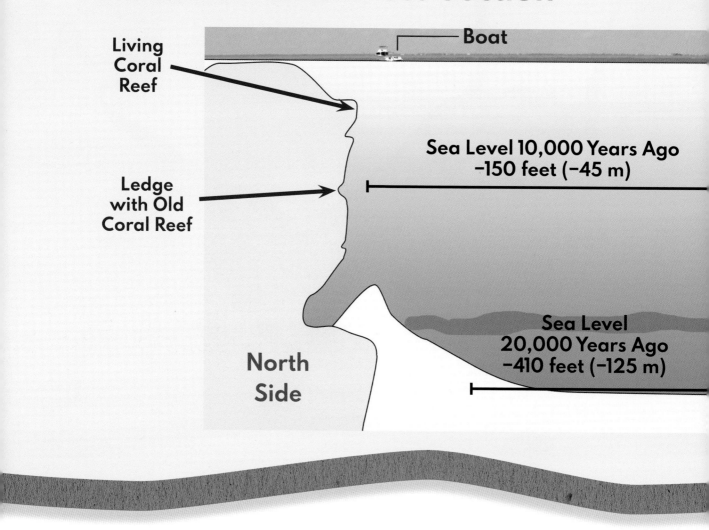

Living Coral Reef

Boat

Ledge with Old Coral Reef

Sea Level 10,000 Years Ago
−150 feet (−45 m)

Sea Level 20,000 Years Ago
−410 feet (−125 m)

North Side

A New Habitat

As sea levels slowly rose, new **habitats** formed

in the sinkhole. There are many ledges of old

coral reefs. Each reef grew and then died once

the sea levels rose too quickly. Then new reefs

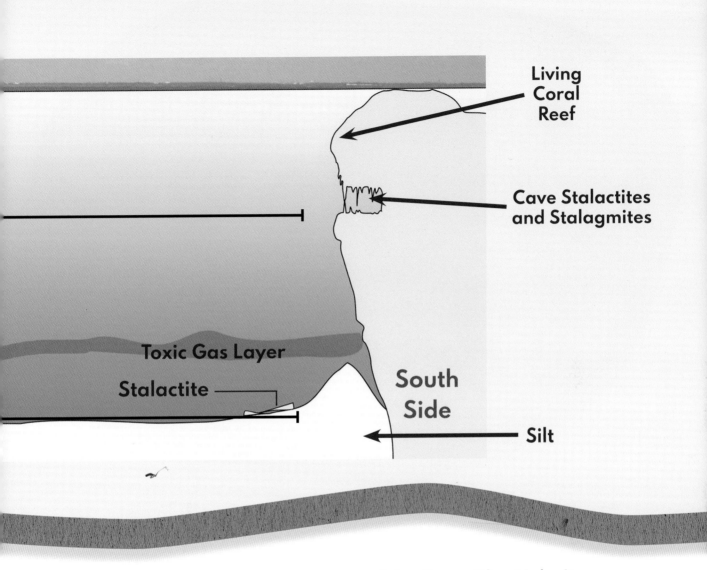

Living Coral Reef

Cave Stalactites and Stalagmites

Toxic Gas Layer

Stalactite

South Side

Silt

This image shows a cross section of the Great Blue Hole. It shows important parts of the hole. Ledges and coral skeletons tell scientists when the ocean levels rose over time.

formed higher up. The skeletons of the old reefs still line the ledges of the hole.

Many species of corals live around the Great Blue Hole.

Today many ocean animals, including corals, make their home at the rim of the Great Blue Hole. The shallow water allows light to filter through to the corals. The light helps the algae that live with the corals grow.

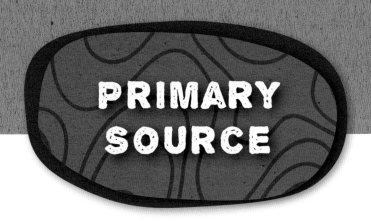

Scientist Erika Bergman explored the Great Blue Hole. She explained how scientists know the hole used to be a cave:

> Stalactites can only form because water is dripping down stone. And so we know that this was a big, dry cave. . . . There [was] probably lots of stuff living in it.

Source: Rebecca Wilkin and Steve Cameron. "Scientists Completed One of the Most Detailed Explorations." *Business Insider*, 1 Mar. 2019, businessinsider.com. Accessed 17 Dec. 2019.

What's the Big Idea?

Read this quote carefully. What is its main idea? Explain how the main idea is supported by details.

Seagrass beds near the Great Blue Hole provide homes for many animals.

CHAPTER 3

LIFE IN THE GREAT BLUE HOLE

The shallow water at the top of the Great Blue Hole is warm and full of light. Reef sharks, fish, and turtles make their homes among the corals near the surface. There are seagrass beds near the hole that turtles feed on.

People snorkel or dive at the Great Blue Hole to see the brightly colored fish and corals. Hammerhead sharks sometimes come into the Great Blue Hole too. People cannot dive to the bottom of the Great Blue Hole. It is too deep. Researchers use submarines to reach the bottom.

A Barrier in the Hole

Plants and animals do not live at the bottom of the Great Blue Hole. There is no oxygen. A layer of hydrogen sulfide creates a barrier. It spreads across the entire hole. The barrier is 300 feet (90 m) beneath the surface.

Snorkelers can enjoy the coral surrounding the
Great Blue Hole.

The algae that lives with corals need sunlight to live, so corals can only grow in shallow water.

Hydrogen sulfide is made when animals and plants die. When **organisms** die, they begin to **decompose**. Oxygen breaks down dead organisms. They release hydrogen sulfide.

Over thousands of years, hydrogen sulfide replaced all of the oxygen in the hole. The chemical creates a cloud that blocks light. Blue holes around the world have this layer.

Ocean waves mix oxygen into water. But the shape of the Great Blue Hole keeps the water inside very still. Very little oxygen reaches the bottom. Once the oxygen was used up, it was not replaced.

A New Life-Form

There are several blue holes around the world. Some of them have bacteria living in the hydrogen sulfide layer. Scientists study the bacteria. They learn about how tiny organisms survive in extreme places.

Conchs are animals with soft bodies. Their shells
protect them.

Animals do not cross the cloud. They need
the oxygen to breathe. If there is no oxygen, they
cannot survive. The bottom of the Great Blue
Hole has the remains of many conchs that fell off

a ledge. Conchs are related to clams and snails. They live in shells. The conchs died because of the lack of oxygen at the bottom of the hole.

Sand and silt are slowly filling in the Great Blue Hole. It is getting shallower over time. The sand and silt become a record of the changing ocean conditions. Scientists continue to study this amazing hole. People around the world admire its beauty.

Explore Online

Visit the website below. Did you learn any new information about coral reefs that wasn't in Chapter Three?

Coral Reef

abdocorelibrary.com/great-blue-hole

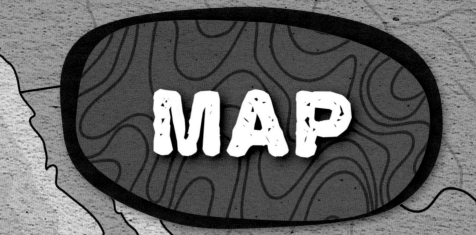

MAP

N
W • E
S

MEXICO

PACIFIC
OCEAN

- Located in Lighthouse Reef off the coast of Belize

- 410 feet (125 m) deep and 980 feet (300 m) wide

- Formed as a dry cave during the last cold period

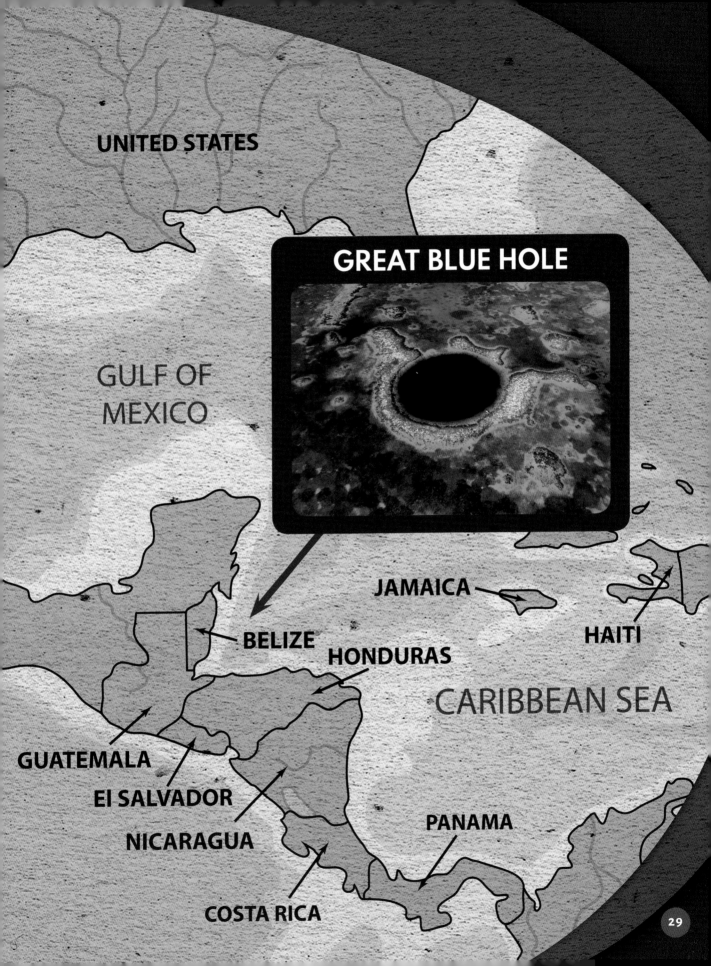

UNITED STATES

GULF OF
MEXICO

GREAT BLUE HOLE

JAMAICA

HAITI

BELIZE

HONDURAS

CARIBBEAN SEA

GUATEMALA

El SALVADOR

NICARAGUA

PANAMA

COSTA RICA

Glossary

coral reef
a long strip of coral that provides a home for many plants and animals in warm, shallow ocean waters

decompose
to break down into smaller parts

habitats
places where plants and animals live

organisms
living things

stalactites
formations made of minerals that hang from the top or sides of a cave and are shaped like icicles

stalagmites
formations made of minerals that rise up from the floor or sides of a cave and are shaped like upside-down icicles

toxic
poisonous to living things

Online Resources

To learn more about the Great Blue Hole, visit our free resource websites below.

Visit **abdocorelibrary.com** or scan this QR code for free Common Core resources for teachers and students, including vetted activities, multimedia, and booklinks, for deeper subject comprehension.

Visit **abdobooklinks.com** or scan this QR code for free additional online weblinks for further learning. These links are routinely monitored and updated to provide the most current information available.

Learn More

Hansen, Grace. *Marine Biome*. Abdo Publishing, 2017.

London, Martha. *Great Barrier Reef*. Abdo Publishing, 2021.

Index

About the Author

Martha London writes books for young readers full-time. When she isn't writing, you can find her hiking in the woods.